The Best of Bob Marley

Cover photo © Fifty-Six Hope Road Music Limited.

ISBN 0-7935-9412-x

HAL•LEONARD®
CORPORATION
7777 W. BLUEMOUND RD. P.O. BOX 13819 MILWAUKEE, WI 53213

Visit Hal Leonard Online at
www.halleonard.com

USING THE STRUM PATTERNS

The songs in this book include suggested strum patterns (Strum Pattern 1.) for guitar. These numbers refer to the numbered strum patterns below.

The strumming notation uses special symbols to indicate up and down strokes.

$$\sqcap = \text{DOWN}$$

$$V = \text{UP}$$

Feel free to experiment with these basic patterns to create your own rhythmic accompaniment.

STRUM PATTERNS

Note: When an (x) is indicated in the pattern, mute the strings.

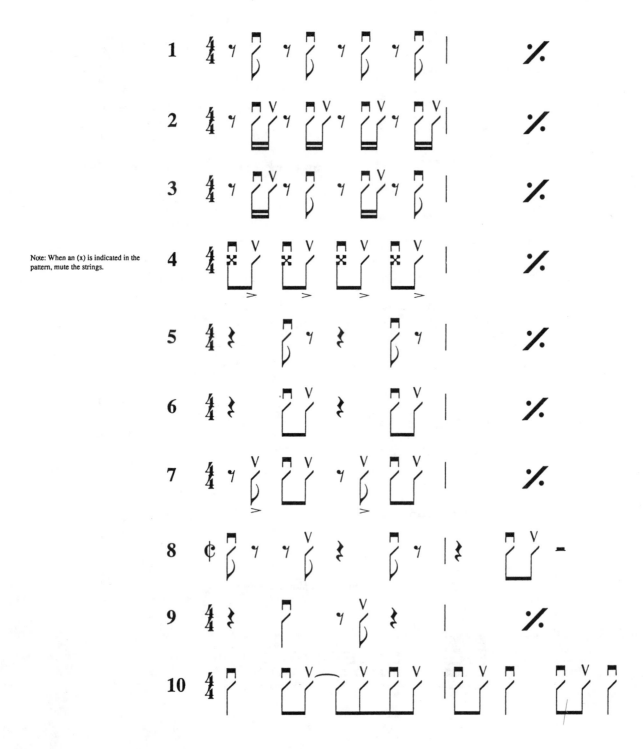

Coming in from the Cold

Words and Music by Bob Marley

Africa Unite

Words and Music by Bob Marley

To Coda ⊕

Chorus

D.S. al Coda

⊕ *Coda*

Outro

w/ voc. ad lib.

Repeat and Fade

Additional Lyrics

2. How good and how pleasant it would be,
   Before God and man,
   To see the unification of all Rastaman, yeah.
   As it's been said already, let it be done, yeah.
   I tell you who we are under the sun.
   We are the children of the Rastaman.
   We are the children of the higher man.

Belly Full
(Them Belly Full (But We Hungry))

Words and Music by Legon Cogil and Carlton Barrett

dance.   For - get your weak - ness and dance.

Cost of liv - ing get so high, rich and poor, they start a cry.

Now the weak must get strong. They say, "Oh, what a trib - u - la - tion."

Them bel - ly full but we hun - gry.   A hun - gry mob is a an - gry mob. _

A rain a fall but the dirt it tough. _   A pot a cook but the food no 'nough. _ We're gon -

na chuck to Jah mu - sic, chuck - in'.   We're chuck - in' to Jah mu - sic, we're chuck - in'.

Chuck - in', _____   chuck - in'. _____

A bel - ly full but them hun - gry.   A an - gry mob is a an - gry mob. _

A rain a fall but the dirt it tough. _   A pot a cook but the food no 'nough. _

Repeat and Fade

Outro

w/ voc. ad lib.

A an - gry man is a an - gry man. _   A rain a fall but the dirt it tough. _

Buffalo Soldier

Words and Music by Noel George Williams and Bob Marley

Outro

Wo, yo, yo, yo, ___ yo, yo, yo. Wo, yo, yo, yo, yo ___

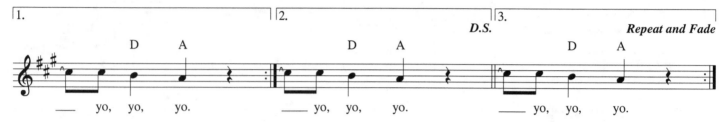

___ yo, yo, yo. ___ yo, yo, yo. ___ yo, yo, yo.

Additional Lyrics

2. And he was taken from Africa, brought to America,
Fighting on arrival, fighting for survival.
Said he was a buffalo soldier, dreadlock Rasta,
Buffalo soldier in the heart of America.

Bridge If you know your history,
Then you would know where you're coming from.
Then you wouldn't have to ask me
Who the heck do I think I am.

5. Trodding through San Juan in the arms of America.
Trodding through Jamaica, the buffalo soldier.
Fighting on arrival, fighting for survival.
Buffalo soldier, dreadlock Rasta.

Chances Are

Words and Music by Bob Marley

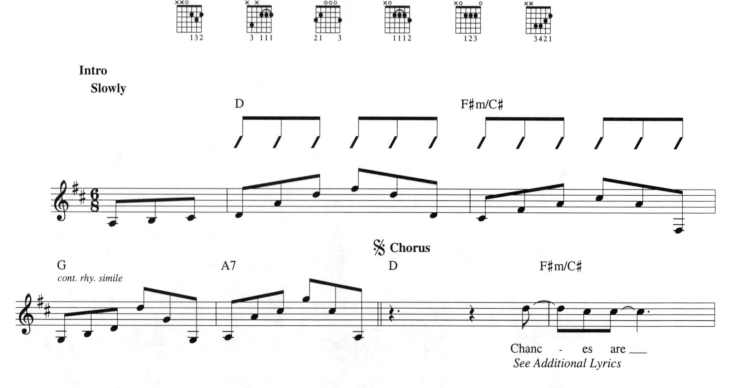

Chanc - es are ___
See Additional Lyrics

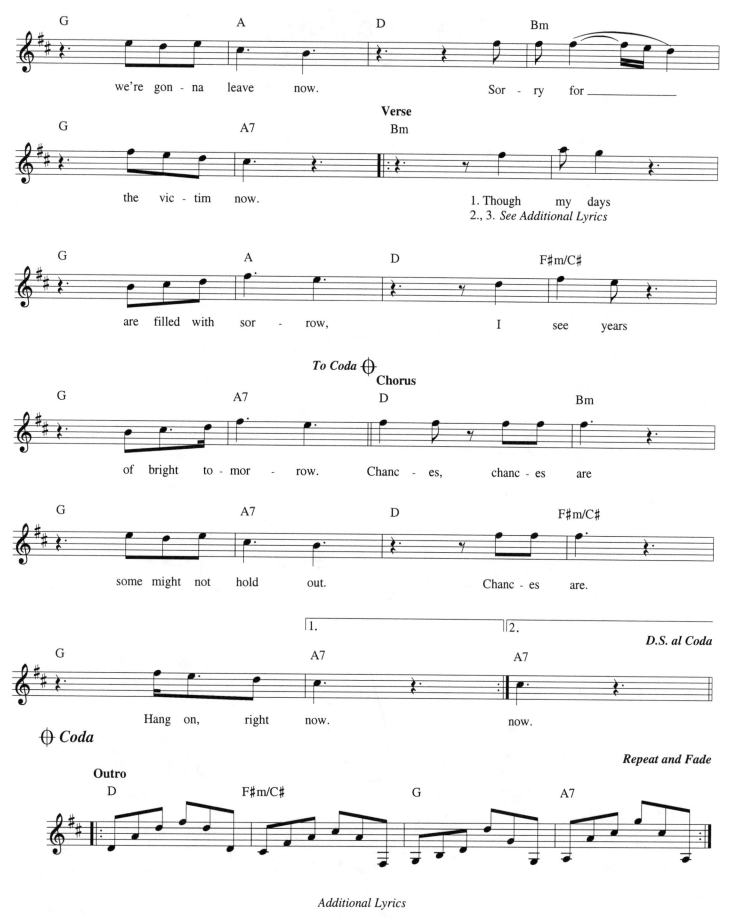

Additional Lyrics

2. Though, though, though, though, though my, my days
Are filled with sorrow.
I see years of bright tomorrow.

Chorus Chances, chances are
Some might not hold out.
Chances are. Hang on, right now.

3. Chances are, oh, chances.
Your my chances.
Chances are. Hang on, right now.

Concrete Jungle

Words and Music by Bob Marley

Strum Pattern: 1

Intro

Moderate Reggae

Verse

1. No sun will shine in my day to-day. (No sun will shine..)
2. *See Additional Lyrics*
3. *Instrumental*

The high yel-low moon won't come out to play. (Won't come out to play.)

Dark-ness has cov-ered my light. (And has changed.) And has changed my day in - to night.

Now where is this love to be found, won't some-one tell me?_ 1., 3. Cause_

Chorus

life must be some-where to be found, yeah. ___ In-stead of a con-crete

2. *See Additional Lyrics*

jun - gle _ where the liv-in' is hard - est. Con - crete

jun - gle, _ oh man, _ you've got to do your best, yeah. _

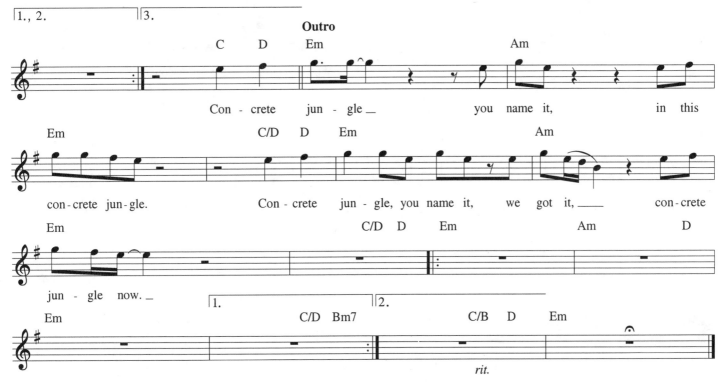

Additional Lyrics

2. No chains around my feet, but I'm not free.
I know I am bound here in captivity.
And I've never known happiness,
And I've never known sweet caresses.
Still, I be always laughing like a clown.
Won't someone help me?

Chorus 2. 'Cause I've, I've got to pick myself from off the ground, yeah.
In this here concrete jungle.
I say, what do you got for me now?
Concrete jungle, oh, why won't you let me be now?

Could You Be Loved

Words and Music by Bob Marley

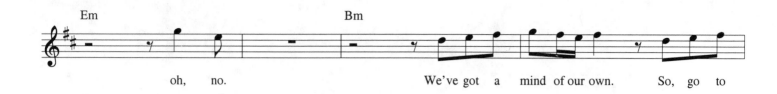

oh,   no.   We've got a mind of our own.   So, go to

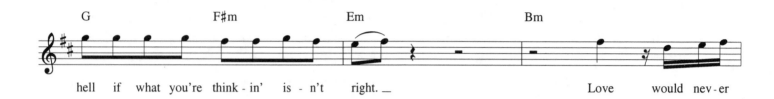

hell if what you're think-in' is-n't right. __   Love   would nev-er

To Coda

leave us a-lone;   in the dark - ness there must come out to   light.

Chorus

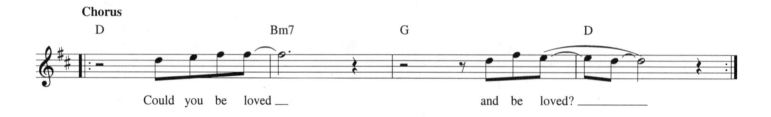

Could you be loved __   and be loved? _____

Interlude

The

road of life is rock - y   and you may stum - ble too. __   So

while you point your fin - gers,   some - one else is judg-in' you.

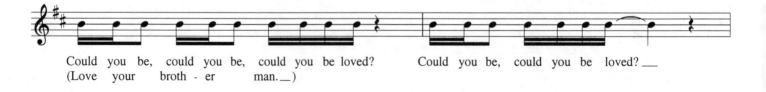

Could you be, could you be, could you be loved?   Could you be, could you be loved? __
(Love your broth - er   man. __)

Could you be, could you be, could you be loved? Could you be, could you be loved? __

Coda

Chorus

Stay a-live, __ oh. Could you be loved __

and be loved? _____ _____ You

ain't gon-na miss your wa - ter un - til your well __ runs dry. No

mat - ter how __ you treat him, the man will nev - er be sat - is - fied.

Could you be, could you be, could you be loved? Could you be, could you be loved?

Repeat and Fade

Outro

w/ voc. ad lib.

Say some-thin', say some-thin'.

Additional Lyrics

2. Don't let them change you
Or even rearrange you, oh, no.
We've got a life to live.
They say only, only, only the
Fittest of the fittest shall survive.
Stay alive, oh.

Crazy Bald Heads

Words and Music by Rita Marley and Vincent Ford

Additional Lyrics

2. Build your penitentiary, we build your schools.
Brainwash education to make us the fools.
Hate is your reward for our love
Telling us of your God above.

Easy Skanking

Words and Music by Bob Marley

Strum Pattern: 5

Intro

Moderately Fast

Eas - y skank - ing, (Skank-ing it eas - y.) eas - y skank - ing. (Skank-ing it slow.)

(Skank - ing it slow.) 1. Ex - (2.)cuse me while I light my spliff. ____ Oh God, ____

____ I've got to take a lift. ____ From re - al - i - ty I just can't drift.

____ That's why ____ I'm stay - in' with this riff. ____ Take it eas -

Chorus

- y. ____ Lord,_ now take it eas - y. Take

See Additional Lyrics

it eas - y. ___ Got __ to take it eas - y. See,

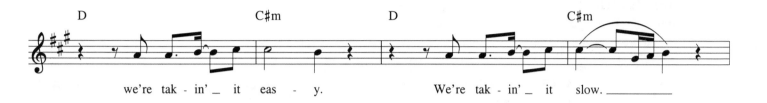

we're tak - in' __ it eas - y. We're tak - in' __ it slow. _____

We're tak - in' __ it eas - y. _____ Got __ to take it slow. So, __ take it eas -

- y. ___ Oh, __ take it eas - y. ___ Take

To Coda ⊕   *D.S. al Coda*

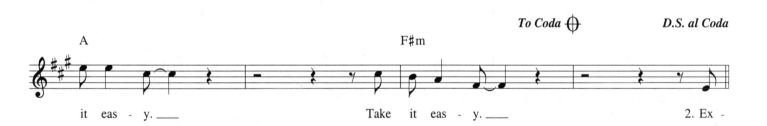

it eas - y. ___ Take it eas - y. ___ 2. Ex -

⊕ *Coda*   *Repeat and Fade*

Outro

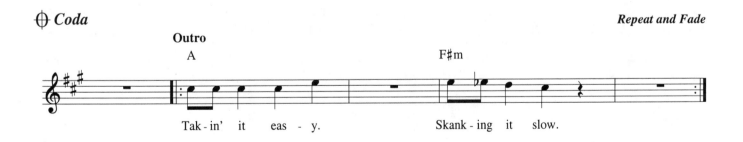

Tak - in' it eas - y. Skank - ing it slow.

Additional Lyrics

Chorus Take it easy. Got to take it easy.
          Take it easy. Skanking, taking it slow.
          Tell you what. Herb for my wine; honey for my strong drink;
          Herb for my wine; honey for my strong drink.
          Take it easy. Skanking it easy.
          Take it easy. Take it easy.

Exodus

Words and Music by Bob Marley

Am7

Strum Pattern: 4

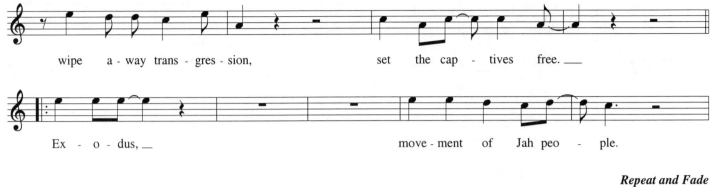

wipe a-way trans-gres-sion, set the cap-tives free.___

Ex - o - dus, ___ move-ment of Jah peo - ple.

Repeat and Fade

Move - ment of Jah peo - ple;

Additional Lyrics

2., 3. Open your eyes, and look within.
Are you satisfied with the life you're living?
We know where we're going.
We know where we're from.
We're leaving Babylon,
We're going to our father land.

Guava Jelly

Words and Music by Bob Marley

Cmaj7 Dm7 G7 C Am F G7sus4

Strum Pattern: 2

Intro

Moderate Reggae

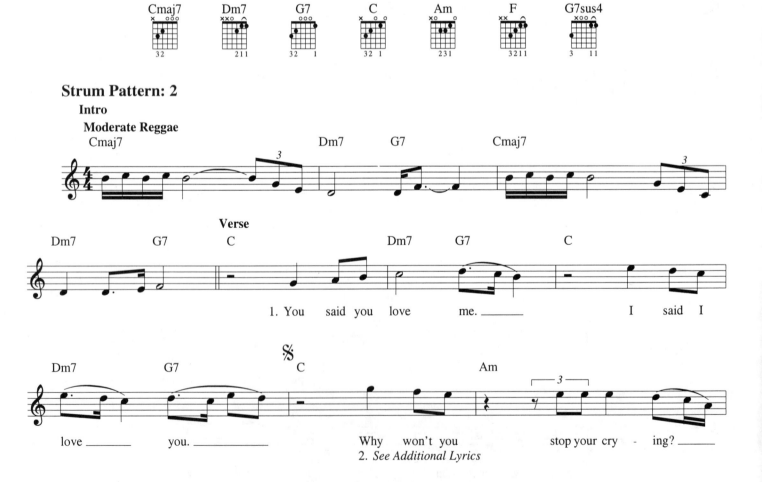

Cmaj7 Dm7 G7 Cmaj7

Verse

Dm7 G7 C Dm7 G7 C

1. You said you love me. ___ I said I

Dm7 G7 C Am

love ___ you. ___ Why won't you stop your cry - ing?___
2. *See Additional Lyrics*

Additional Lyrics

2. I'll say you should stop, stop crying.
   Wipe your weeping eyes.
   You'll see how I'm gonna love,
   Love you from the bottom of my heart.

Get Up Stand Up

Words and Music by Bob Marley and Peter Tosh

I know you don't _ know what _ life is real - ly worth. _ Is not all _

_____ that glit - ters is gold? ___ And half ____ the sto - ry has nev -

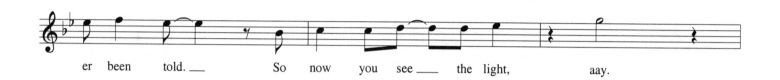

er been told. ___ So now you see ____ the light, aay.

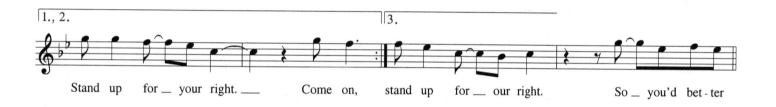

1., 2.   **3.**

Stand up for _ your right. ___ Come on, stand up for __ our right. So _ you'd bet - ter

Outro-Chorus

Cm

{ get / Get } up, stand up, stand up for ____ your right.

Repeat and Fade

Get up, stand up, don't give up ____ the fight.

Additional Lyrics

2. Most people think great God will come from the sky,
   Take away ev'rything, and make ev'rybody feel high.
   But if you know what life is worth,
   You would look for yours on earth.
   And now you see the light.
   You stand up for your right, yah!

3. We're sick and tired of your ism and skism game.
   Die and go to heaven in Jesus' name, Lord.
   We know when we understand. Almighty God is a living man.
   You can fool some people sometimes,
   But you can't fool all the people all the time.
   So now we see the light. We gonna stand up for our right.

I Shot the Sheriff

Words and Music by Bob Marley

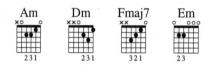

Strum Pattern: 8

Additional Lyrics

2. Sheriff John Brown always hated me;
   For what, I don't know.
   Every time that I plant a seed,
   He said, "Kill it before it grows,"
   He said, "Kill them before they grow."

3. Freedom came my way one day,
   And I started out of town.
   All of a sudden, I saw Sheriff John Brown
   Aimin' to shoot me down,
   So I shot, I shot, I shot him down.

4. Reflexes had the better of me,
   And what is to be must be.
   Ev'ry day the buckett a-go-a well
   One day the bottom a-go drop out
   One day the bottom a-go drop out.

I'm Hurting Inside
(Hurting Inside)

Words and Music by Bob Marley

Strum Pattern: 1, 3

Intro

Reggae Rock

Verse

1. When I was just _____ a lit - tle child,
2. *See Additional Lyrics*

hap - pi - ness _____ was there a - while.

Then from me, yeah, _ it slipped one day. _____

Hap - pi - ness, come back, I say. _____ 'Cause if you

Pre-Chorus

don't come I've got to go look - in' for hap - pi - ness. Well, if you

don't come, I've got to go look - in', Lord, for hap - pi - ness, hap - pi - ness.

Chorus

I'm hurt - ing in - side. _____

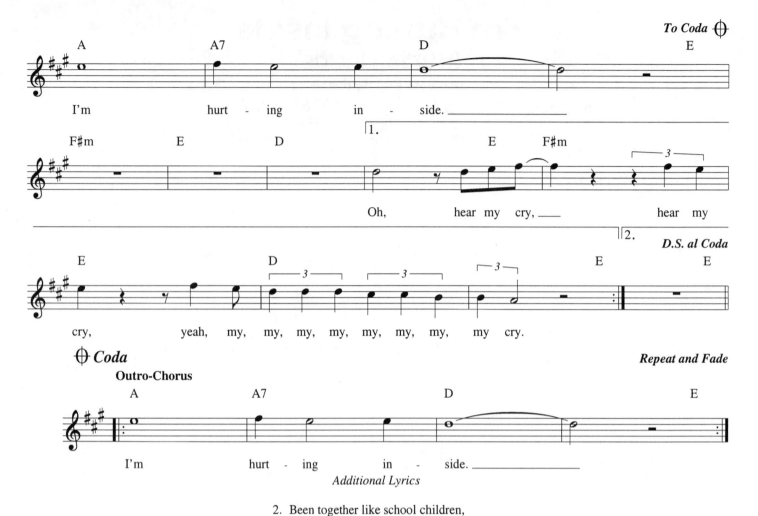

Additional Lyrics

2. Been together like school children,
   Then you hurt me just in vain.
   Lord, I'm your weary child.
   Happiness, come back awhile.

I'm Still Waiting

Words and Music by Bob Marley

Strum Pattern: 9

Additional Lyrics

2. Why, girl, oh, why, girl?
   You know, you know I love you.
   That's why I wait my whole life through.
   My parting to you for being what I am.
   But don't you know I'm waiting?

Iron Lion Zion

Words and Music by Bob Marley

Additional Lyrics

2. I'm on the run, but I ain't got no gun.
   See, they want to be the star,
   So they fighting tribal war.
   And they saying, "Iron, like a lion, in zion.
   Iron, like a lion, in Zion."
   Iron, lion, Zion.

4. I'm on the run, but I don't got no gun.
   See, my brothers want to be the stars,
   So they fighting tribal war.
   And they saying, "Iron, like a lion, in Zion.
   Iron, like a lion, in Zion."
   Steal them off of me. Iron, lion, Zion.

Is This Love

Words and Music by Bob Marley

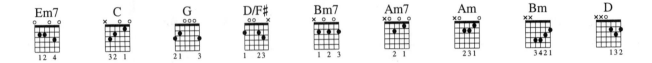

Strum Pattern: 5

Intro

Moderate Reggae

1. I wan - na love

Verse

(2., 3.) you   and treat you right. ___   I wan - na love

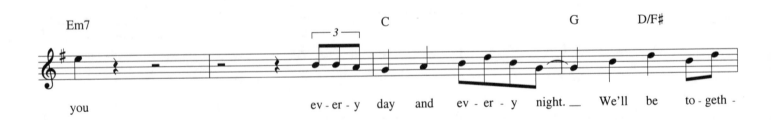

you   ev - er - y day and ev - er - y night. ___ We'll be to - geth -

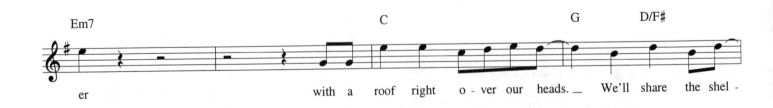

er   with a roof right o - ver our heads. ___ We'll share the shel -

Jammin'

Words and Music by Bob Marley

Strum Pattern: 4

jam - min', jam - min'. We're jam - min' right straight from yard. ____

Interlude

Ho - ly Mount _ Zi - on; Ho - ly Mount _ Zi - on.

Jah sit - teth in Mount Zi - on and rules ____ all

D.S. al Coda

cre - a - tion. Yeah, we're we're jam - min'. 4. Bop - chu - wa - wa -

✛ *Coda*

Outro

w/ voc. ad lib.

jam - min', jam - min'. I wan - na jam it with you. ____ We're

jam-min', we're jam-min', we're jam-min', we're jam-min', we're jam-min', we're jam-min', we're jam-min', we're jam-min'.

Repeat and Fade

Hope you like jam - min', too. ____ We're

Additional Lyrics

Chorus 2. We're jammin'.
   To think that jammin' was a thing of the past.
   We're jammin',
   And I hope this jam is gonna last.

2. No bullet can stop us now, we neither beg nor we won't bow
   Neither can be bought nor sold.
   We all defend the right, Jah Jah children must unite,
   For life is worth much more than gold.

Chorus 4. Bop-chu-wa-wa-wa. We're jammin'.
   I wanna jam it with you.
   We're jammin',
   And jam down, hope your jammin', too.

3. Jah knows how much I've tried, the truth cannot hide,
   To keep you satisfied.
   True love that now exists is the love I can't resist,
   So jam by my side.

Kinky Reggae

Words and Music by Bob Marley

Outro

w/ voc. ad lib.

eh!   Kink - y,   kink - y reg - gae.

Additional Lyrics

2. I went down to Piccadilly Circus;
Down there I saw Marcus.
He had a candy tar
All over his chocolate bar.
I think I might join the fun, (I might join the fun.)
But I had to hit and run. (Had to hit and run.)
See I just can't settle down (Just can't settle down.)
In a kinky, kinky part of town.

Chorus Nice one; that's what they say, (Nice one.)
But I'm a-leavin' you today. (Nice one.)
Oh, darlin', please don't play: (Nice one.)
Mama say, mama say.
Kinky reggae, kinky reggae, uh!
Kinky reggae, now! Take it or leave it!
Kinky reggae, believe it! Kinky reggae, now!
It's kinky reggae, it's gonna be kinky reggae!
Kinky reggae, now! Cuka-yeah, now!
Kinky reggae. Sca-ba-dool-ya-bung, baby!
Kinky reggae, now, oh, oh, ooh!
(Ride on!) Ride on! Come on, yeah!
(Ride on!) Riding on, riding on!
Ride on, kinky reggae. Come on, ride on! Eh, eh!

Nice Time

Words and Music by Bob Marley

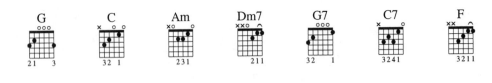

Strum Pattern: 1

we no have no nice time, doo yoo-dee-dun-doo, yea. Think a-bout that.

Bridge

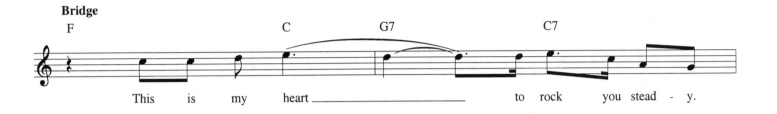

This is my heart _____ to rock you stead - y.

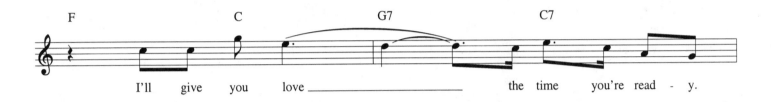

I'll give you love _____ the time you're read - y.

This lit - tle heart __ in me just won't let me be.

Verse

I'm just to rock you, now. Won't you rock with me? 2., 4. Long time

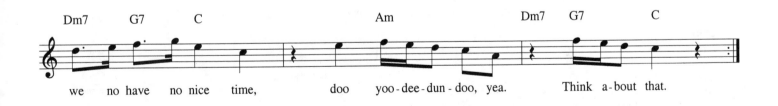

we no have no nice time, doo yoo-dee-dun-doo, yea. Think a-bout that.

Repeat and Fade

Outro

Lick Samba

Words and Music by Bob Marley

up a - lick it one time, right there. ___ Whoa, _____ lick sam - ba. ___ I'll ___

Verse

___ set - tle the lit - tle a claim, _ ba - by. 2. You can write it down in my name, _____

morn - ing time, noon or night. _____ A - just - a -

Chorus

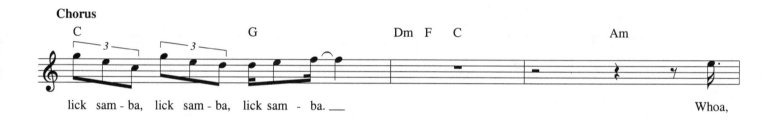

lick sam - ba, lick sam - ba, lick sam - ba. ___ Whoa,

now. Yeah! _____ Oh, dar - ling.

If it's morn - ing time, I'm _ read - y. And if it's late at night, I'm _ stead - y.

D.S. and Fade

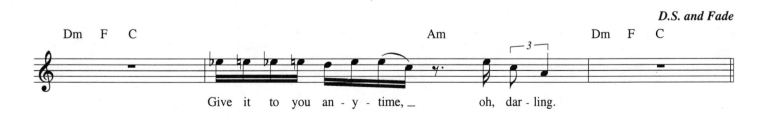

Give it to you an - y - time, _ oh, dar - ling.

43

Lively Up Yourself

Words and Music by Bob Marley

No Woman No Cry

Words and Music by Vincent Ford

good friends_we had __ oh good friends we've lost _ a - long the way._

___ In this bright fu-ture you can't for-get your past

so, dry your tears _ I _____ say. And __ through, but while I'm gone I mean...

Interlude

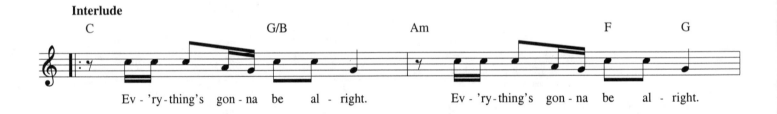

Ev - 'ry-thing's gon - na be al - right. Ev - 'ry-thing's gon - na be al - right.

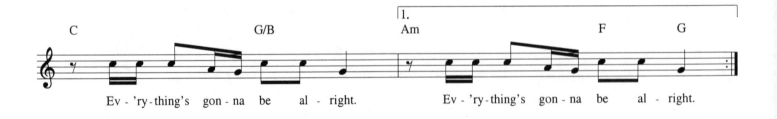

Ev - 'ry-thing's gon - na be al - right. Ev - 'ry-thing's gon - na be al - right.

Ev -'ry-thing's gon - na be al - right so, wom-an, no cry. No, no

wom-an, no wom-an, no cry. Oh, my lit-tle sis-ter don't shed no tears._

Additional Lyrics

2., 3. Said I remember when we used to sit
In the government yard in Trenchtown.
And then Georgie would make a firelight
As it was logwood burnin' through the night.
Then we would cook corn meal porridge
Of which I'll share with you.
My feet is my only carriage,
So, I've got to push on through, but while I'm gone I mean...

Mellow Mood

Words and Music by Bob Marley

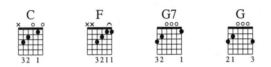

Strum Pattern: 3

Intro

I'll play your fav'r-ite song, dar-lin'. We can rock it all night

Chorus

long, dar-lin'. 'Cause I've got love, dar-lin, love, sweet

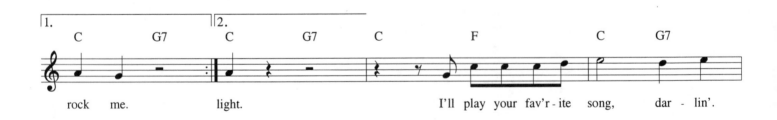

love, dar-lin. { Mel-low mood has got me, so let the mu-sic
{ Qui-et as the night, please turn off your

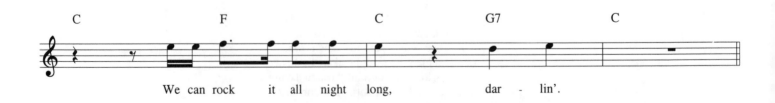

1. rock me. 2. light. I'll play your fav'r-ite song, dar-lin'.

We can rock it all night long, dar-lin'.

Natural Mystic

Words and Music by Bob Marley

Strum Pattern: 5

Intro

Moderate Reggae

Am7

There's a nat-'ral mys-tic blow-ing through the air. ___ 1. If you

Verse

lis-ten care-ful-ly ___ now, you will hear. ___ This could

2. *See Additional Lyrics*

(3.) be the first trum-pet, might ___ as well be the last. ___ Man-

y more will have to suf-fer, man-y more will have to die. ___

___ Don't ___ ask me ___ why.

Chorus

1. *Things are not the way ___ they used to be. ___*

2., 3. *See Additional Lyrics*

Additional Lyrics

2. One and all got to face reality now.
   Though I try to find the answer
   To all the questions they ask,
   Though I know it's impossible
   To go living through the past.
   Don't tell no lie.

Chorus 2. There's a nat'ral mystic blowing through the air.
   Can't keep them down.
   If you listen carefully now, you will hear.
   Such a nat'ral mystic blowing through the air.

Chorus 3. There's a nat'ral mystic blowing through the air.
   I won't tell no lie.
   If you listen carefully now, you will hear.
   There's a nat'ral mystic blowing through the air.

No Sympathy

Words and Music by Bob Marley

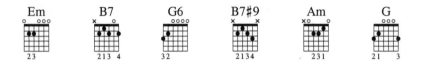

Strum Pattern: 6

Intro

Moderately Slow

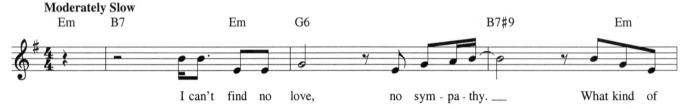

I can't find no love, no sym-pa-thy. __ What kind of

love they got for me? __ I'm on __ my way __ to hap-pi-

ness where I __ can find __ some peace and rest. __

%. Verse

1. When I'm in my trou-bles, yeah, __ on-ly me __ feels __ the pain, __
2. *See Additional Lyrics*

__ the sad-ness. Not __ one sim-ple word, __ good word of ad-vice from

One Drop

Words and Music by Bob Marley

Feel it in the one drop and we'll still ___ find time ___ to rap.

We're mak-ing the one ___ stop, { the gen - er - a - tion gap. and we fill in the gap. }

So, feel this drum beat as it beats with - in,

play - ing a rhy - thm { re - sist - ing a - gainst the sys - fight - ing a - gainst i - sm and }

- tem. Ooh - we, } I know JAH'd nev - er let us down. ___ Pull your rights ___
ski - sm.

One Love

Words and Music by Bob Marley

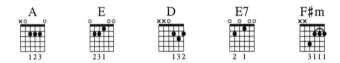

Strum Pattern: 1

Intro
Relaxed Reggae Beat

Chorus

One love, ___ one heart. ___ Let's get to-geth - er and

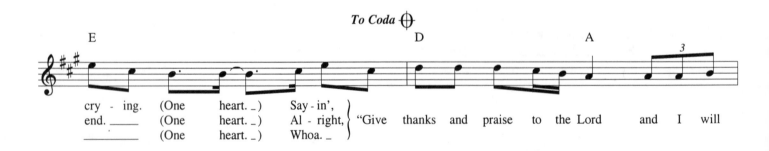

feel all right. { As it was in the be - gin - ning, (One love. ___) so shall it be in the
I'm plead - ing to ___ man - kind. (One love. ___) Oh, Lord. ___

Hear the chil-dren cry - ing. (One love. ___) Hear the chil-dren

To Coda

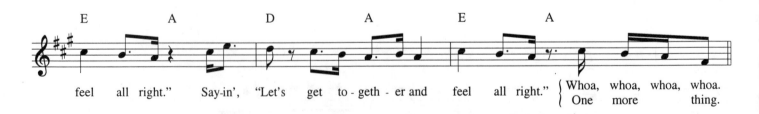

cry - ing. (One heart. ___) Say - in',
end. ___ (One heart. ___) Al - right, { "Give thanks and praise to the Lord and I will
___ (One heart. ___) Whoa. ___

feel all right." Say-in', "Let's get to - geth - er and feel all right." { Whoa, whoa, whoa, whoa.
One more thing.

Verse

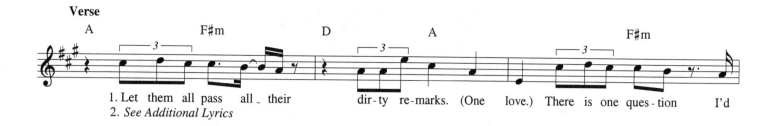

1. Let them all pass all their dir-ty re-marks. (One love.) There is one ques-tion I'd
2. *See Additional Lyrics*

real - ly love to ask.__ (One heart.) Is there a place _ for the

hope - less sin - ner who has hurt all man - kind just to

save his own?__ Be - lieve me. Fath - er of Cre - a - tion. Say - in',

Coda

Outro-Chorus

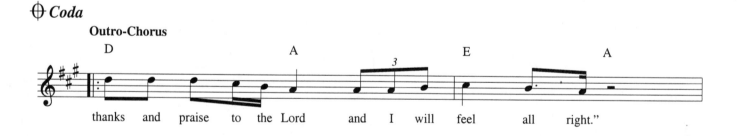

thanks and praise to the Lord and I will feel all right."

Repeat and Fade

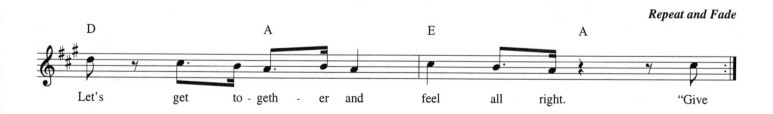

Let's get to - geth - er and feel all right. "Give

Additional Lyrics

2. Let's get together to fight this Holy Armageddon, (One love.)
So when the man comes there will be no, no doom. (One song.)
Have pity on those whose chances grow thinner.
There ain't no hiding place from the Father of Creation. Sayin',

Pimper's Paradise

Words and Music by Bob Marley

Strum Pattern: 6

Verse

Moderately Fast

got an e - go to feed.   Whoa, ___ a

⊕ Coda

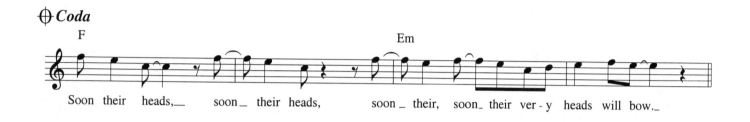

Soon their heads,___ soon ___ their heads,   soon ___ their, soon ___ their ver - y heads will bow.___

Outro-Chorus

Pimp - er's ___ par - a - dise,   don't lose track,   don't lose track of your - self, ___   oh ___ no!

Repeat and Fade

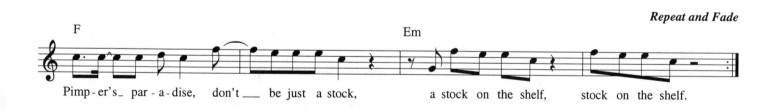

Pimp - er's ___ par - a - dise,   don't ___ be just a stock,   a stock on the shelf,   stock on the shelf.

Additional Lyrics

2. She loves to model, up in the latest fashion.
   She's in the scramble and she moves with passion.
   She's getting high, trying to fly the sky.
   Now, she is bluesing when there ain't no blues.

Please Don't Rock My Boat

Words and Music by Bob Marley

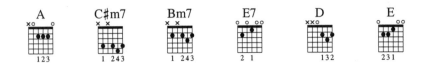

Strum Pattern: 1

1. Please don't you rock my__ boat, __ 'cause I

don't want my boat to be rock-in' an-y-how. Please don't you rock-a my

boat, ____ no, _ 'cause I don't want my boat to be rock-in'. 2. I'm tell-in' you that

oh, oo, oh, I like it a like a this. Can you miss?
3. *See Additional Lyrics*

And you should know, ooh, oh, when I like it a like a

this,   I'm a real - ly   is,   ooh, yeah.   You sat - is, sat - is,

sat - is - fy my soul till morn - ing time. Ev - 'ning goes. _ Sat - is - fy   my   soul. Yes, I been a

tell - in' you.   Bake me the sweet - est cake _   hap - py in - side   all   the

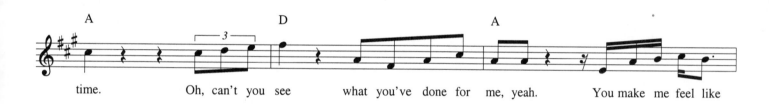

time.   Oh, can't you see   what you've done for me, yeah.   You make me feel like

when we bend a new cor - ner.   We feel like   sweep - stake win - ners, yeah.

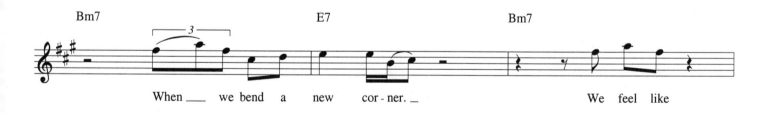

When __ we bend a   new   cor - ner. _   We feel like

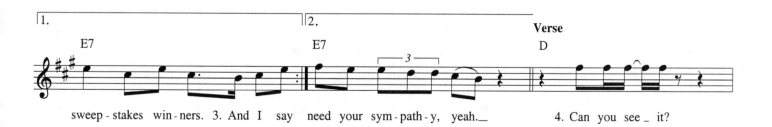

sweep - stakes win - ners. 3. And I say   need your sym - path - y, yeah. _   4. Can you see _ it?

Do you be - lieve_ me?   Oh, dar - lin', dar - lin',   I'm call - in', call - in'.

Sat - is - fy my soul, _   sat - is - fy my soul. _   Nev - er, nev -

Outro

- er, nev - er give it up now.   We're all in the same boat,

rock - in' on the same rope.   We've got to get to - geth - er,   lov - ing each

oth - er.   And can't you see   what I've got for you, yeah.

Repeat and Fade

I'm hap - py, hap - py, hap - py, hap - py, hap - py, hap - py, and not e - ven time to be blue, yeah.

Additional Lyrics

3. And I say oh, oo, oh, I like it a like a this.
   Yes, I do. And you should know, ooh, oh,
   When I like it a like a this, I've got it.
   Just can't miss, ooh.
   You satisfy my soul, darlin'.
   Make me love you in the mornin' time, yeah.
   If ever I treated you bad,
   Make it up to you one time.
   'Cause I'm happy inside all the time.
   I want you beside me, yeah, to be mine.
   One thing you got to do, when we are holding hands together,
   You've got to know that we love, we love each other, yeah.
   And if ev'ry time you should walk away from me,
   You know I need your sympathy, yeah.

Roots, Rock, Reggae

Words and Music by Bob Marley

Redemption Song

Words and Music by Bob Marley

Strum Pattern: 10

Intro

Moderately

N.C.

1. Old

Verse

G   Em7   C   G/B   Am

pi - rates, yes, they rob I.   Sold __ I __ to the mer-chant ships __

2., 3. *See Additional Lyrics*

G   Em   C   G/B   Am

min - utes af - ter they __ took I   from the bot-tom - less __ pit. But my

G   Em7   C   G/B

hand _____ was made __ strong   by the hand of the Al - might -

Am   G   Em

- y.   We for - ward in this gen - er - a - tion __

C   D

tri - umph - ant - ly.   Won't you help to sing __

Additional Lyrics

2., 3. Emancipate yourselves from mental slav'ry,
None but ourselves can free our minds.
Have no fear for atomic energy,
'Cause none of them can stop the time.
How long shall they kill our prophets
While we stand aside and look?
Some say it's just a part of it.
We've got to fulfill the book.

Small Axe

Words and Music by Bob Marley

These__ are the words of my mas-ter. Keep on tell-ing__ me
2nd time, Instrumental

no weak__ heart shall pros-per, oh, no they can't. __ 3., 4. And

Verse

who-so-ev-er dig-geth a pit, Lord, shall fall in it, shall

fall in it. Who-so-ev-er dig-geth a pit shall

1.

2.

bur-y in it, shall bur-y in it. If you are the bur-y in it. If you have a

Outro-Chorus

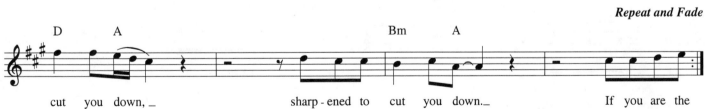

big tree __ we {have a / are the} small __ axe, __ read-y to

Repeat and Fade

cut you down, __ sharp-ened to cut you down.__ If you are the

Additional Lyrics

2. I say you're working iniquity to achieve vanity, yeah,
But the goodness of Jah Jah endureth forever.

So Much Trouble in the World

Words and Music by Bob Marley

Additional Lyrics

2. We've got to face the day.
   Ooh wee, come what may.
   We the street people talking.
   We the people struggling.
   Now, they're sitting on a time bomb.
   Now I know the time has come.
   What goes on up is coming on down.
   Goes around and comes around.

Soul Captive

Words and Music by Bob Marley

Strum Pattern: 1

Intro

Moderately

1., 3. Tra, la, la, la, la, la.   Tra, la, la, la, la, la.

2. *Instrumental*

Soul cap-tives are free. _____   Tra, la, la, la, la, la.

Tra, la, la, la, la, la.   Soul cap-tives are free.   1., 2. When you

Verse

wake up ear-ly in the morn-ing,   and you

work like dev-ils in the sun,   time _____ slips a-way with-

out warn-ing   but sweet-er day _____ will come.

Soul Rebel

Words and Music by Bob Marley

Waiting in Vain

Words and Music by Bob Marley

78

I don't wan-na, I don't wan-na, I don't wan-na, I don't wan-na, I don't wan-na wait in vain. __ It's your

Outro

Repeat and Fade

love that I'm __ wait-ing on. It's my love that you're run-ning from. __ It's your

Additional Lyrics

2. It's been three years since I'm knockin' on your door,
And still can knock some more.
Ooh girl, ooh girl, is it feasible,
I wanna know now, for I to knock some more?
Ya see, in life I know there is lots of grief,
But your love is my relief.
Tears in my eyes burn, tears in my eyes burn
While I'm waiting for my turn.

Who the Cap Fits

Words and Music by Aston Barrett and Carlton Barrett

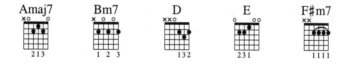

Strum Pattern: 6

Intro

Verse

1. Man to man is so un - just, _____ chil -
2. *See Additional Lyrics*
3. *Instrumental*

dren. You don't know __ who to trust.

Your worst en - e - my could be your __ best friend, __

and your best friend __ your worst en - e - my.

Instrumental Ends

Some will eat and drink with you.
Some will eat and drink with you.

Then be - hind them __ su - su 'pon you.
Then be - hind them __ su - su 'pon you.

On - ly your friend know your se - crets, _____ so on -
And if your night should turn to day, _____ a - lot

ly he could re - veal it. }
of peo - ple would run a - way. } And who the

Chorus

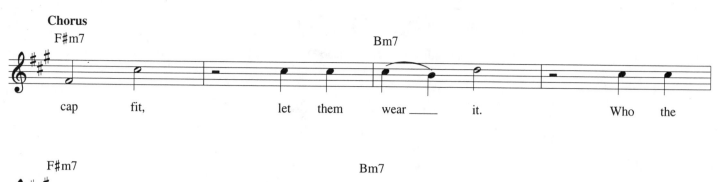

cap   fit,   let   them   wear ____ it.   Who   the

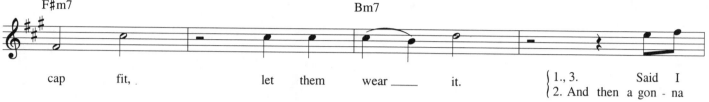

cap   fit, ___   let   them   wear ____ it.   { 1., 3.   Said   I
                                              { 2. And then a gon - na

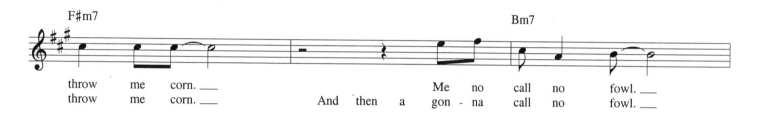

throw   me   corn. ____   Me   no   call   no   fowl. ____
throw   me   corn. ____   And   then   a   gon - na   call   no   fowl. ____

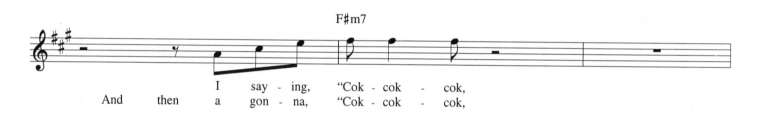

I   say - ing,   "Cok - cok - cok,
And   then   a   gon - na,   "Cok - cok - cok,

cluk, cluk, cluk,"   yea.   cluk, cluk, cluk."   I   say - ing,

Repeat and Fade

Outro

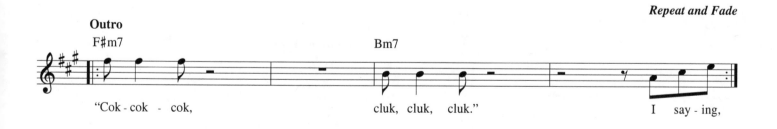

"Cok - cok - cok,   cluk, cluk, cluk."   I   say - ing,

Additional Lyrics

2. Some will hate you, pretend they love you, now.
   Then, behind they try to eliminate you.
   But who Jah bless, no one curse.
   Thank God, we're past the worse.
   Hypocrites and parasites
   Will come up and take a bite.
   And if your night should turn to day,
   A lot of people would run away.

Stir It Up

Words and Music by Bob Marley

To Coda ⊕

Additional Lyrics

2. I'll push the wood, I'll blaze your fire,
Then I'll satisfy your, your heart's desire.
Said I'll stir it, yeah, ev'ry minute, yeah.
All you got to do, honey, is keep it in.

3. Oh, will you quench me while I'm thirsty?
Or would you cool me down when I'm hot?
Your recipe, darling, is so tasty,
And you sure can stir your pot.

Sun Is Shining

Words and Music by Bob Marley

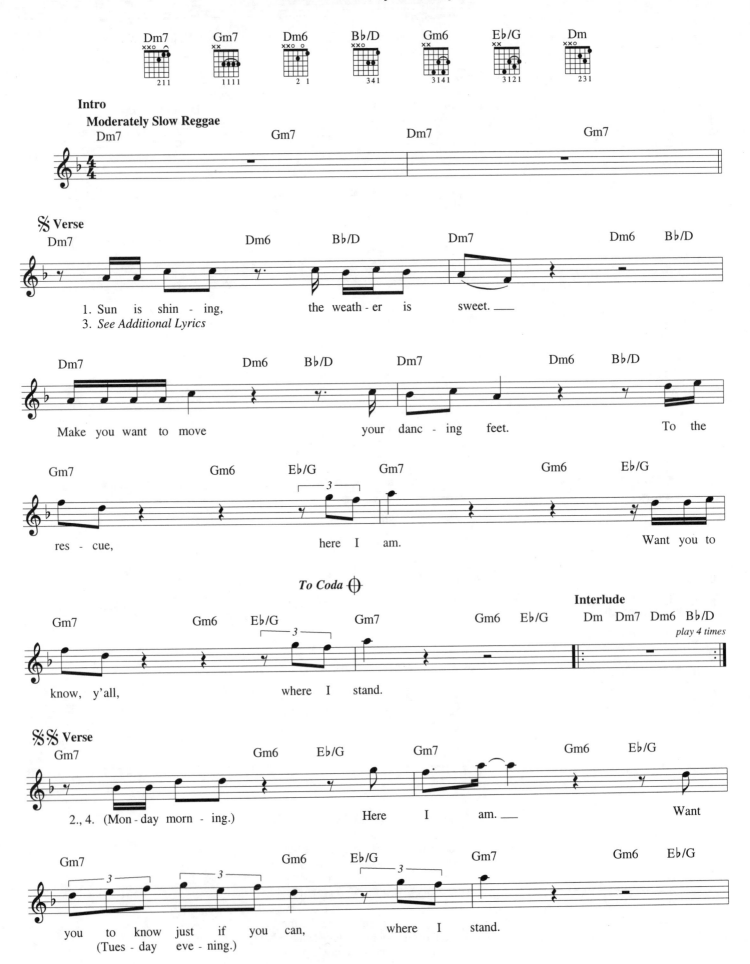

res - cue,   here I am.   Want you

D.S.S. and Fade

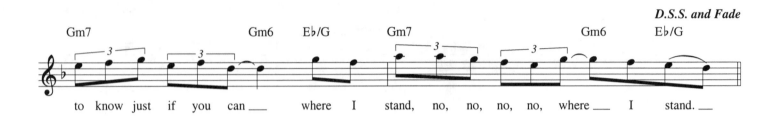

to know just if you can ___ where I stand, no, no, no, no, where ___ I stand. ___

Additional Lyrics

2. When the morning fog gathers the rainbow,
   Want you to know I'm a rainbow, too.
   So, to the rescue, here I am.
   Want you to know just if you can,
   Where I stand, know, know, know, know, know, know, know, know.

Three Little Birds

Words and Music by Bob Marley

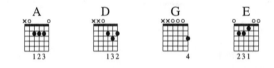

Strum Pattern: 2

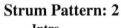

Intro

Moderately Slow

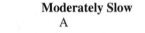

Don't

Chorus

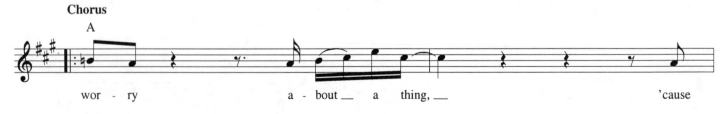

wor - ry   a - bout ___ a thing, ___   'cause

Thank You Lord

Words and Music by Bob Marley

Strum Pattern: 7

Intro
Bright Reggae

Thank you, Lord. _____

Chorus

Thank you, Lord, for what you've done for me. _____

Thank you, Lord, for what you're do - ing now. _____

Thank you, Lord, for ev - 'ry lit - tle thing.

Thank you, Lord, for ev - 'ry song I sing. __

Verse

1. Say I'm __ in no __ com - pe - ti - tion,
2. *See Additional Lyrics*

but I made my de - ci - sion.

Additional Lyrics

2. Said I can't find the explanation, Lord, have mercy,
To prove my appreciation.
Lord, in my simple way, yes,
I am a-comin', comin', comin', comin'. I love to pray.

Time Will Tell

Words and Music by Bob Marley

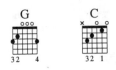

Strum Pattern: 1

D.S. al Coda

tree,   saw the free-dom tree.   Saw you set-tle the score.   Oh, chil-dren weep no

more.   Weep no more,   chil-dren weep no more.   4. JAH would nev-er

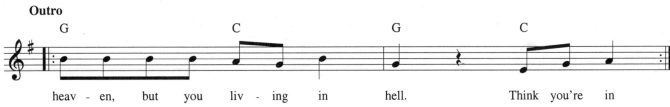

⊕ *Coda*

Repeat and Fade

Outro

heav-en, but you liv-ing in hell.   Think you're in

Trench Town Rock

Words and Music by Bob Marley

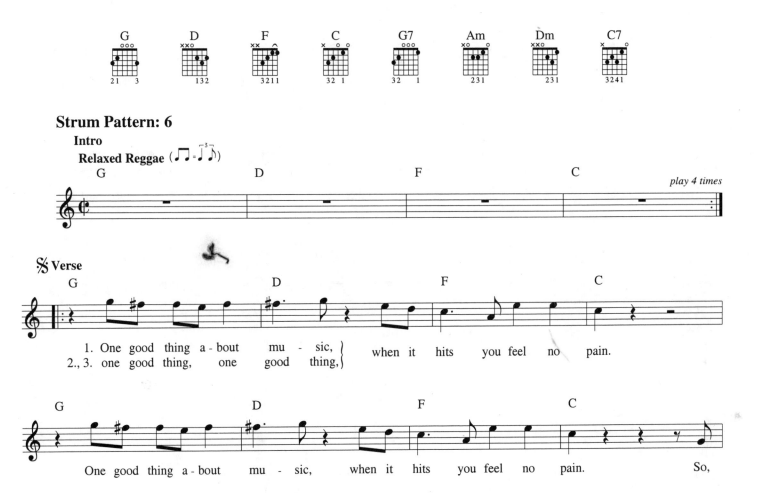

Strum Pattern: 6

Intro

Relaxed Reggae

play 4 times

Verse

1. One good thing a-bout   mu-sic,   } when it hits   you feel   no   pain.
2., 3. one good thing,   one   good thing, }

One good thing a-bout   mu-sic,   when it hits   you feel   no   pain.   So,

Why Should I

Words and Music by Bob Marley